Math Basics

Counting Cars

By Nick Rebman

www.littlebluehousebooks.com

Little Blue House is distributed by North Star Editions:
sales@northstareditions.com | 888-417-0195

Produced for Little Blue House by Red Line Editorial.

Photographs ©: iStockphoto, cover, 7 (bottom), 9 (bottom), 11 (top), 13, 16 (top right), 16 (bottom right); Shutterstock Images, 4 (top), 4 (bottom), 7 (top), 9 (top), 11 (bottom), 15 (top), 15 (bottom), 16 (top left), 16 (bottom left)

Library of Congress Control Number: 2020900744

ISBN
978-1-64619-165-9 (hardcover)
978-1-64619-199-4 (paperback)
978-1-64619-267-0 (ebook pdf)
978-1-64619-233-5 (hosted ebook)

Printed in the United States of America
Mankato, MN
012021

About the Author

Nick Rebman enjoys reading, walking his dog, and traveling to places where he doesn't speak the language. He lives in Minnesota.

Table of Contents

Counting Cars

I count two cars.

The cars are blue.

I count three cars.

The cars are orange.

I count four cars.

The cars are red.

I count five cars.

The cars are white.

I count six cars.

The cars are yellow.

I count seven cars.

The cars are gray.

Glossary

blue

white

orange

yellow

Index